D0356768

SLOW DANCING AT MISS POLLY'S

SHEILA ORTIZ TAYLOR

The Naiad Press Inc.
1989

Printed in the United States of America
First Edition

Cover design by Phoenix Graphics
Typesetting by Sandi Stancil

Library of Congress Cataloging-in-Publication Data

Taylor, Sheila Ortiz, 1939—
    Slow dancing at Miss Polly's.

    I. Title.
PS3570.A9544S64 1989   811'.54   88-29123
ISBN 0-941483-30-4 (pbk.)

About the Author

Sheila Ortiz Taylor was born in Los Angeles in 1939, when the sun, Mercury, and Venus were all playing kneesies in Libra. This conjunction may have given her an inclination to indecision but she's not sure.

As a child she wore six-guns, brought home stray cats, and had an imaginary playmate. In elementary school she learned to garden and square dance; in junior high, to prefer gym teachers to imaginary playmates; in high school to prefer English teachers to anything.

Degrees adhere to her. Together with her B.A., M.A., and Ph.D., Taylor boasts a certificate in motherhood granted by the Middletown Connecticut Red Cross and a yellow belt in Judo, signifying the rank of Roku (which translated means "The Weakling").

Her two daughters having safely passed through the battle zone into adulthood, Taylor now lounges through life teaching creative writing to young geniuses, fishing with her partner, and eating chocolate chip cookies in secret.

Works by Sheila Ortiz Taylor

Acknowledgments

Acknowledgment is made to the following publications for poems that originally appeared in them:

Apalachee Quarterly: "The Author to Her Former Husband"
Broomstick: "Mid-Life Love"
Common Lives/Lesbian Lives: "Dyke Patrol"
Sinister Wisdom: "Southern Exposure"

In memory of my mother

Contents

Part I: Album

Part II: Dyke Patrol

Part III: Sunday Morning

PART I:
Album

How to Please Your Mother

It was a hot day in the valley.
The rabbits panted behind wire,
tongues lolled
out of the dogs
sprawled like bathmats
on the cool wood floor

It looked like the right place to be.
I might disguise myself as a dog
by the time my mother paid her visit
to her grown
cowering daughter
mother of two

The clock said there was no time for that
too late for strategies.
The drill sergeant's tires now
rolled hot on four lane asphalt
toward me,
at fault

My children danced safe at Miss Polly's.
They played with the pre-school goat
and ate Campbell's noodle soup from Mr. Ted's kitchen

I unzipped my dog suit and hitched up an apron.
I rode the Hoover around the rumpled rug
stripped the kitchen floor

re-grouted the shower
dusted the dogs
fed Coke bottles down the garbage disposal
while the cat picked up toys
and the rabbit ate the false aurelia

Almost time.
Imperial tire tracks
on the off-ramp
Ventura Freeway north.
I tossed back a glass of Lysol
and stared into my closet
lazering along with my mother's eye
to find what would please her

Listen.
I speak to you now as a survivor.
I stood there a long time.
The cat kept tugging on my pant leg.
I asked the question into my closet:
What would please her?
It took a while before I could hear the answer:
Nothing

And isn't that enough?
Time now to zip on your dog suit
and boogie on down to Miss Polly's

Certifiable

Now I know
I am crazy.
Sliding a blind hand down
this dark hall
moon in Capricorn
3 AM
feeling my way
around
the queen size
sofa bed
plump with sleeping guests
past the puzzled dog
one eye open
to my study
where
without spectacles
without light
I write
this poem.

35MM

This poem is a camera.
Pick it up
and fit it to
your face.
Let your eye
walk through
the view
finder
and frame
your scene.

Check for light.
Verify distance.
Focus with care.
Press the button.
I am the film.

Album

I

She stood in the doorway
leaning in
a hibiscus behind her ear
my father in the kitchen
changing lightbulbs

Look at her hands.
There are maps
in her hands
polish on each tipped finger
like a lurid kiss
not given

She stands in the doorway
hips aslant
watching hummingbirds
kiss the hibiscus
by the door

Lady of the olive trees
palace-bound
beneath humming
high-tension wires

My father
on the ladder

has carefully unscrewed
the large kitchen globe
gently turned the darkened bulb
so as not to smash
it
screwed in the new
refitted the globe
climbed backwards down
to where
moving a hand to his damp brow
he finds his tinted glasses
holding the dark
against afternoon sun

Dinner. In we come
down from late summer trees
my sister and I
half-afraid
edging down
to a mother-and-father life
a table with dribbling glasses
of milk growing warm
and steak growing cold
of candles sinking onto
the polished table top

Now, says my father,
whatever you want,
ask for it in Spanish.
The hibiscus lady's eyes
dark as olives on the tree

rise rafter-high
and we squirm

My sister's untutored elbow
seeks a glass
to knock over.
In a river of milk
she drowns all our sins
(pray for us now
and at the hour)

Mantequilla. We leap
for towel and mop
while he sits
trying to remember the Spanish
for patience

At last we sit back down
my sister and I
studying her face
like a dictionary
relinquishing forever
the idea of butter with dinner
we watch our
hibiscus lady through tinted lenses

II

He wanted to sail.
She wanted to spin.

9

One day we drove to Long Beach
our faces pressed into backseat triangles
carsick
restless to be
out of sight
up a tree

At last we pulled into a boatyard
where sailboat carcasses
rested on skystilts
reached only by ladder
and hungry vision

There, he said pointing.
My sister and I
raised our sails
tacking toward his dream

But my mother wanted a fur coat
instead.
She hung back
denied the ladder
slept fitfully
woke
with fur in her mouth

For two years
we sanded
painted
watched stars at night

shot them with sextants
quadrants
compasses
fixed them

A truck came and bit the boat
slunk off
carrying it seaward in his mouth.
My father
driving behind
laboring in his mind
saw
not the launch
and swing of champagne
but phantom sloop strewn
across the Long Beach Freeway
Southbound

My mother
in the back seat
knitting her words
in sharp white needles
screamed at last
in flawless Spanish
until the boat swung out over
water
and failed
to sink

The Way Back

for Uncle Jim

They stand in this Christmas snapshot
poised like adagio dancers
facing each other
their arms draped around
their matching bones
brother and sister
while behind them
out of focus
the family
spins

Around
these two,
youngest of thirteen,
held now for eternity
in this moment before their
twin feet slide them out in a
celestial tango,
a silence gathers

We see their handsome faces
Indian bones in glinting cheeks
their raven hair, grey-streaked
their eyes as deep and dark as wells
holding a history of careless loss:
land, lovers, mothers, maps.

The way back is a land
more innocent than this.
He joined the navy; she married a judge.
They both baked bread in institutional ovens.
He wrote long letters home
and sent his mother silk pillows
embroidered with military targets.

He baked bread while
his eight brothers lost fingers
toes, knees, elbows.
He could almost hear the bullets
thud into dough
and the sound made him rise
growing from uniform to
uniform until they had to declare peace

Home again he folded away his whites
kissed his sisters and told his brothers
he was going to become a hair dresser.
This made their wounds ache
more than seemed possible.
Finally he followed them to work at Lockheed
and learned to drill holes in himself
discovered insomnia
married a beautician named Molly
whose hair he dyed green every Christmas

He loved all holidays.
Life needed themes
spelled out

in sparkles, sprinkles,
cut-outs, paste-ups,
but most of all
in costumes

Halloweens found brother and sister
on their knees before bolts of cloth
and wimpling tissue
pins in their mouths
blue chalk on their hands
for years
artists of the self

You can see it
here in this snapshot —
white polyester pants
belling out around
white cowboy boots
red western shirts
tailored close to the rib
Indian silver at the waist
twins in spirit
if not by birth
they, holding each other
in a light embrace
their grace not lost

And yet,
the way back is a land
more innocent than this.
The time came round

when neighbors,
preferring razor blades to invention,
would not let their children trick
or treat where a grown man
put costumes on

His eyes turned to silver.
That Christmas night, very late,
he backed his throbbing
Continental into the dark garage
that shut down tight behind him
and crawled into the back seat
bearing a bottle of champagne
one glass
a photograph

Doncella 109: A Guest House in Puerto Rica

I

This shall suffice.
Magnificent on her wicker throne
she leans forward
dispensing egg rolls and calm.

Monarch of quiet
we know you.
You are the form
who waits in the door
disputing nothing
awaiting our return.

II

9:00 A.M.
Down the hall with orange juice and Ovaltine
she comes
the jangler with a tale of —
what was it? —
oh yes, the old lady captain
with a wooden leg
who married at sea
the first mate to his monkey.

16

She it is who makes French toast
glaring into the griddle
until touched by the Muse
whose ass she pretends to pinch.

Storyteller, jangler, fool
loved for your gifts
of incidental truth
we know you.

III

The queen waves her hand
beckoning the jester.
Under these moon-glaring trees
we stand as if in ceremony,
under these moon-glaring trees
we see the form in the doorway
embrace the wise fool.
The queen of silence knows
this shall suffice.

What Mrs. Fish Said

It was that Mrs. Fish
sits in the sun room
afternoons
with the Raggedy doll
in her lap
whilst others
wheel off to their rooms
to steal naps
and bury old bones

It was me seen her granddaughter coming
the one from Minnesota
this one
all new looking
carrying upside down
a bed jacket somebody back home knitted
all wrapped up in tissue paper
and tied with blue ribbon

Mrs. Fish stares, see
like one of them Cousteau fish
underwater
surprised
to be
on T.V.

This lady
Mrs. Fish

with
tissue paper skin
and little blue lines
leading
toward secret air

this lady smiles
letting go words
that swim
like minnows in schools
toward the niece

this lady saying kindly
"Life's strange"
then she leaning close to the girl
me leaning over the information counter
clamping the space to my ear
like a shell
to hear her say
"Life's very strange —
specially when *you're* strange"

Conveyer

We tied on white aprons
and put brown spidery nets
over our heads
banged shut lockers
filled with talk
and scraped up the stairs
to the floor

Buns were coming off
Great trays whacked
by bakers' hands slid
them down the belts
in a spray of sesame seeds
and stories

I walked past
smiling self-consciously
at my Aunt Rosie
whose nodded chin
pointed me out
with pride
to the bun girls

Past cakes
in chocolate and vanilla
swirls
my Aunt Thelma
in the thick

wielding her own
three-stroked knife
discussing with the cake girls
the Happy Hooker
and on
to pies

One thing we must not do:
stash food
in that obliging apron bulge
just below our girlish breasts
There must have been other things
we must not do
but we never inquired

On this particular day
just before Christmas
I think
when giddy with labor
we had packed in the
Feffernut cookie tins
notes saying HELP
we are prisoners
in Van de Kamp's bakery

On this day
filled with ourselves
bulges grew
girl by girl
below each breast
Until we exploded

at break time
down the staircase
hurling
from hip and shoulder
pies at every face
and back
fruit slathering
everywhere
laughter
breaking through nets

Marker

They said her ashes
were strewn over the desert
from an airplane at sundown
but I could remember photographs
in my dentist's magazine
of glowering FBI agents
shouldering into black cars
pilots whose rose gardens
had been enriched by their
unprotesting clients

In her only recorded comment on death
my mother leaned across
the Palm Springs breakfast table
we two shared alone
and said of her dead friend,
"They put her out like the trash.
Not a word in the paper. Nothing."
Coffee cup to her lips
she stared out the kitchen window
through bougainvillaea and grill work
to desert sand and mountain beyond.

One day she turned to bones
on contour sheets.
I flew all day
from Florida
changing planes

in every time zone
my watch winding backward

My sister and I sat in shifts
and dripped water into her open
mouth through straws
while my father crouched
under his desk
selling life insurance

Relieved at sunset
we walked
through orange groves
swam together
through the darkening pool
listening to the wind
sawing off the limb of night

Once my mother saw
girls in white dresses
dancing on the lawn
Next she saw her mother
standing at the foot of her bed
beckoning

But she clung to her kitchen table
said No to her mother
tuned in to "The Price is Right"
watched through lids
that kept dropping

like storefront
grills

One day she dropped her remote control
turned away from Bob Barker
and asked, "Is that all there is?"
"Yes," I lied,
holding her
drawing her
toward death,
like a midwife
pulling a child
toward the light

For days that passed for years
we dripped morphine
into her gaping mouth
and wandered through the failing house
while time pulsed through the clocks
and out her veins

Then one night the burglar stood
just beyond her locks
His razor circled the window once
and glass fell out
He stuffed her jewels into pillowcases
slashed photographs with razors
stole the television
and the light

I held her tight.
"Go to your mother," I said.
"You go," she answered
and turned away.

Next morning
I watched her turn into a spot on the sheet.
We folded her like a flag
and gave her to the pilot.
She lives now in petal and thorn.

Airstream

There was a gypsy camp
called The Silver Lake Auto Court
at the foot of my father's mountain
It was cool in there
and dark too
I went, selling Girl Scout cookies
pulling a Radio Flyer full of my wares
before the fear of Tylenol
and rape made us all middle aged

Trailers like somnolent silver fish
lay side by side
ignoring amiably
the people inside
sawing through their dinner
the people outside
sitting on camp stools
and broken kitchen chairs
the woman with the watering can
crooning to her window boxes
the man in his undershirt tying up tomatoes

Come in, they would say
throwing wide the ripped screen door
and drawing me into breakfast nooks
of ripped red naugahyde
feeding me cookies, home made,
and milk from jelly glasses

then releasing me into the stream
again like a fish too small
until the next hand drew me in
set me on the kitchen counter
called to Fred in a back bedroom
did he have three quarters

All this must have violated my father's
sense of zoning
Bad enough the PA system
that assaulted his ears
calling nomads to the phone
in strangled tones
at all hours

And now his daughter
free as a fish
he could not quiet reel
he could not quite feel
exactly what it was drawing her at sunset
away from the mountain
toward barking chihuahuas
and squalid houses with wheels

My father has slept in marble these thirty years
survived by his gypsies
who have grown double-wide
and own touchtone phones
I watch them through his study window
my telescope pressing past the security guard

but their blinds are down hard
they give at the office

Sometimes in the night though I wake
stubborn as a Girl Scout
and search for signs of secret life
I have seen them once or twice:
as if summoned to a phone
they rise from crazy beds
pour through the screendoor
in their pajamas
moving as easily
as a fish through water
and begin
casting off:
clotheslines
trellises
dog houses
green houses
carports
satellite dishes

The hitch is cold in your hands now
I grip the wheel
turn the key
watch for the guard
We edge forth
lights flashing
engine panting like a heart —
giving ourselves to the airstream

PART II:

Dyke Patrol

Equal Access

Your calls are always collect
and from another time zone.
Breakfasting in my sleep
at a Zurich sidewalk cafe
you leap to a pay phone
drop your silver coin
into my mouth
reversing the charges
to say you are thinking of me

Which is hard to believe
and expensive.
You have dialed
over time
into the dreams
of six sweet lovers
sent them all packing
looking vague in their pajamas
as they waited for the bus

Last month my phone bill was 30,000 pesetas
and one more lover.
Yes, the dollar has fallen
a dime at a time
for half my life
my bill swelling and deflating
like taxed lungs

while you lay on the beach
at Nice

But, listen, my wrong number:
the rates are down now
and equal access prevails.
This is your order to
disconnect.

After the Beep

I never wanted
an answering machine.
Like Gertrude Stein
I always thought,
"What is the question?"
not "What is the answer?"

But my friend said
she liked them,
that when you called
an answering machine,
left your message,
then you could draw a line
through another obligation.

Out of courtesy
I mastered the impossibilities
and charged on my Diners' card
an Execu-phone.

Last Saturday
it came
in a brown stapled box
with limited guarantees
and limited instructions,
mostly in Korean.

It is important not to panic
before the partially assembled.
I worked quietly
half the night
with my screwdriver
electrical tape
and Korean dictionary.

Next day from work
I called my house
(This is a test).
The line was busy
all afternoon.
When I went home
that night
there were
no messages.

Last night
rather late
the phone rang.
My own recorded voice
calling collect
greeted me from London.
I did not leave a message.

Minimum Wage

He had clean-shaven jaws
and wore a thick, brown apron
over houndstooth trousers

He paid me a dollar and twenty-five
cents an hour to find the customers'
shoes and put them in brown paper bags
and take their money

There were tickets with numbers
and a mountain of desolate shoes
made new by this clean-shaven man
smelling of shoe polish and burning rubber

Sometimes late afternoons
I would clean the front window
and stack the polish tins
in high, improbable pyramids

At five I would wave good-by
stroll through Clock Town where
crazy Mr. Smith sat all day
in a white booth
overseeing clocks on posts
white graveled walks
benches where no one sat
and three pay phones

Then across the Hyperion Street Bridge
up the red clay cliff
smelling of earthworms
edging carefully past the cave
where once two dirty boys had said
to my sister and me
Wanna fuck?
and finally home

One day the man in jaws
sitting on his work bench
eating a bologna sandwich
at lunchtime
leaned forward
baring teeth
breathing whiskey
sipped from the crumpled bag
he kept

Listen he said
pointing at a Coca-Cola
calendar on the wall
behind me
See her?
She looks like you

She was laughing
in her make-up
throwing her head back
so her neck stretched
long and pink

and her yellow hair fell
backward
and her mouth fell
open for Coke

I was fourteen.
I ran through Mr. Smith's Clock Town
across the Hyperion Street Bridge
up the red cliff
and sat in the cave
until it was time to go home

Dyke Patrol

This was long ago
when you were afraid to park your car
outside the bar.
They could do things.
It was not safe.

This happened in LA
Six bikers
zipped into black jackets
not looking like diamonds
on black velvet.
They held beer in brown bottles
and their jaws in hard lines.

They had come to demonstrate
their irreproachable sexuality
in the parking lot of the women's bar.
A kind of flashing, I guess.

Three women in the parking lot
paused, waiting
a fourth said, Who the shit do you think
you are?
A fifth made a phone call.

I leaned against the hard line of my car
in the night
I can remember the fog soaking into my

shoulder through my jacket,
the one with no zippers.

I wondered why I had come
and if my shrink had been right when she said
to get out and meet some people,
stop using up her Kleenex
twice a week
waiting for a heart to seal up
and be well again.

It seemed that night
in the waiting
that anything might happen.
A brown bottle could graze
my heart
I might bleed to death in an
alien parking lot
among strangers.

What I was waiting for was this.
A white car
with welts all over its body
a car — it seemed — with sixteen doors
all popping open at once
while the scorched squeal was still
in the air
from angry tires
and sixteen dykes striding toward
six bikers
backing off

backing down
moving back in space
moving back to the tune of
my healing heart.

When You Moved In

When you moved in
you brought your dog
and then your sister
who slept on my floor
in a velour bathrobe
a large ashtray
of dead cigarettes
set up like tombstones
by her head

The dog rose early
completing the trash man's route
before he could even wipe the sleep
away

But I saw
black plastic bags
agape
ravaged
strewn
crazily with eggshells
and coffee grounds
across my neighbors'
slumbering lawns

Your sister slept late.
Getting ready for work
we stepped around her.

When we came home
she was tired
of T.V.
and hungry too

I fed her.
I fed the dog.

At night
in my dreams
I knocked over garbage cans
ripped black sacks
without mercy
kneeled at the ashtray
beside your head

This morning
I watched
your finger
linger
on the snooze button
like a dreaming passenger
waiting for a bus

Instead of stepping
around
your sister and her ashtray
you packed them
in ziplock
The dog too.

Afterward I ate ice cream
out of the carton
standing at the kitchen window
licking rocky road
from a deep
cold
spoon

Interiors

Sometimes the mind
is a bat cave
where blind screams
careen
and airlift up
on sudden drafts

Later
radar turned low
each settles quiet
on crowded ledge
rodent head
folded in a black fan

Art Gum

Listen,
this could erase.
If some cosmic hacker
pushed Apple Delete
and nobody had made any
hard copy or back-up disks
of this and nobody knew
how to boot anymore
then compatible
would not be enough.

47

The Author to Her Former Husband on the Occasion of His Growing Misfortune and Her Accomplished Indifference: An Epistle

I used to think it was all my fault
(well wasn't it?)
when for example the rusty Ford
station wagon caught fire
at midnight
just outside Hot Pots, Utah
and it was raining too
(the baby, three months old, had colic)
and the fireman wrapped her in his Levi jacket
and did Humphrey Bogart imitations
all the way to the fire station

You accused me of having a good time

I should have brought your black umbrella
a fire extinguisher
a 50,000 mile warranty
a copy of Dr. Spock
the Book of Mormon

Now, twenty years later —
believing in the power of gifts,
not events —
I publish novels in which you appear
in an ungraceful light.
Your daughter

in shining boots and a yellow slicker
travels by hook and ladder

One thing I know:
nothing is as sure as justice,
or as slow.

Jaws

Outside my study door
the dog dreams
in peace
her white paws giving an occasional
canter across her landscape
of canine pleasures

She does not dream
at 4 pm I planned
her murder
step by step
for the thirty-ninth time
I think

It began with an occasional shoe
round holes in t-shirts you put on
the stuffed bear's ear

At two months she ate the corduroy couch
at three months devoured a table leg
then, the ultimate —
white bites right
through sheetrock
chewing through
from one room
to the next
in a flash of jaws
nobody saw

It would happen
the experts said
within ten minutes
of our leaving.
Turn on the T.V.
they said:
game shows calm the mind

But she put us in jeopardy
beat the clock
dialed for dollars
and all with jaws

One day she ate mini-blinds
in the morning
and every screen
by dusk

One evening she ate the elbows
out of my friend's
snappy blue wool jacket
the one with the Navy buttons

Once she ate a ring
fallen off the finger of a fat guest
who stayed too long.
Rage and madness
are not always liabilities
I suppose

I watch her dreaming now
this dog
of mine
in seeming death
untroubled by half-digested
coffee grounds
moldy cheese
waxed paper
lapped yogurt
Tarot cards
murder plots

And when she rises from her death-sleep
shakes her collar
yawns benign teeth
and seeks my hand
I let it fall
soft
on her soft head

PART III:

Sunday Morning

Naming

Our selves, said Virginia Woolf,
are many, like a tall stack of plates
on a waiter's hand:
one self comes forth
only if Mrs. Jones is gone,
another if it rains.
Some selves, I think, we know
when others name them

Tiz, for instance
a name given to me
by the first son of two lesbians,
a boy born by midwife in the woods
while we leaned all night on the hoods
of our cars drawn up in a circle.
Tiz was the part of Ortiz that could
fit through his mouth.
The self he named remains
eats ice cream
delivers babies

Crispy is the name my lover gave
when I survived in a single year
divorce, earthquake, flood,
Anglo-Saxon, and her own loss

Mama Joe, my children called me when
they filled the house with friends
and laughed to see me feed them all

Lerdy was my sister's word
a skinny girl who wears pigtails
skins her knees,
eludes her mother
who calls her Shell

Some names are secret names
we give ourselves
like Fluff the Bengal Tiger
a secret self of a serious friend
highly placed
whose Fluff-self snorts
and tells crude jokes

But there are other names
bestowed, almost
earned, perhaps
in this way:
one day
pulling grocery bags
out of the truck
I paused to watch a hawk
rise on the blue wind
and loft himself almost
beyond my mind
and then another flew
and sketched an equal path

a third then
and each hawk completing
the same design
until the sixth rose
and fell against
a final blank sky.

I call myself Six Hawks.

Confessions of An Escape Artist

Loving you is a matter
of muscle and marrow
tendon and bone
of cells dividing
in the dark hallways
of self

You could tell me to leave.
I would pull down my brown
canvas bag
throw in the model galleon
my father made
sitting on the back stoop
of a falling down house
in west Texas
throw in my IRS returns
for the last seven years
my socks
my fortune cookie
my Old English Sheep Dog
my Visa card
with the receding limit

I could do all this.
I could throw this bag in the back
of my truck
gun my engine
till it sobbed

release the emergency
back out
in a blue cloud
drive to west Texas
and still I would not
be gone

Mid-Life Love

Do you remember
when you learned to paint
in Mrs. Beardsley's kindergarten class?

Do you remember
yourself
in your father's old shirt
the arms cut off
leaning over orange juice cans of
fragrant calcimine?

Do you remember when she split
your world
with news that
faces
were not pink
that skies
instead of floating
touched the ground?

Tonight, love, I tell you
the skies float purple
and the green calcimine tiger
eats alive
our Mrs. Beardsley

We lie in one another's arms
now

belly to scarred belly
pink again
loving ourselves alive —
artists once more

Star Trek

Sometimes there is a quiet in you
like the quiet in space
where stars breathe

Sometimes there is a rhythm in you
unsyncopated as starfall
on an accidental night

Sometimes there is a space in you
galaxies could not hold,
if you know what I mean

I have seen you launch,
rockets on fire,
the countdown of heart
and splitting sound —
me on the ground
growing smaller

Playing Possum

Saturday morning —
sun slits silent through blinds
striping the sheet
under which we curl
like sleeping puppies.
I play possum
moving closer so that the blood
snoozing through you
accepts me sleepily into its
circling current.

You move back into my warmth
using me like the chair I become.
Holding you against imagined dangers
I grow fierce and able
half-wish for a charging cougar
a crazed boar
to shoot
and then resurrect
with the memory
of your soft sounds
from the evening before
the flickering candle
the open window
the open door.

You wake now
to your imaginary alarm

and then, more quietly
to this still Saturday.
You place your finger
to my lips in warning.
If we make a noise
the dogs will wake
and bark and caper
in the kitchen
till we rise and take
them out.
We lie now in each other's arms
quietly guarding time
as if death itself
were a dog in a distant room
waiting to solve her loneliness
at the first sound of life.

Southern Exposure

We sit silent
side by side on the couch
before this waning fire
in the house we have made
with our own hands
and my mind dreams down
like a diver descending
until I reach the rippled
fill beneath
strewn with bent nails
and bits of blue chalk
then sinking down further
to the slope of native earth
gone pale like a wound too long
covered

The day the truck backed up
and spilled the sand
into golden breasts
we knew we had begun.
We drew rooms with sticks
had pizza delivered
and slept sound in the
invisible house

We took a long time
in the depressions of sand
handling the smooth plastic

pipes like ancestral bones
we laid down for eternity

When the concrete ran like lava down the chute
and into our forms
you said you believed in concrete.
I wanted to write sonnets just there
where the moon had spilled her sepia face.
You said you believed in sonnets too:
we made love in wet cement
and slept in the bathtub
under the tree

We who had never measured anything before
believing in concrete and sonnets
awoke with tape measures in our hands
reckoned square feet
cubic feet, running feet,
sawed lumber into blocks
that miraculously fit
drilled holes
snapped lines
chalked hieroglyphics
on beams
and at last
raised the creature's bones

In Florida heat
our feet sticking to black tar
we nailed the roof

moving slow
like moon-walkers in space

Inside, we grew used
to seeing through walls
to passing sandwiches
and wry comments
through airy division
to kissing between studs
sweet as a forest

We delayed sheetrock
put your old blue rug
on the living room floor
and perched on nail keg chairs
drinking coffee.
Your mother brought a plant
laughed at our "southern exposure"

Then the rains came.
We hurried
hoisting the heavy sheets
bending in our hands like damp cardboard
their chalky innards wanting to spill
and return to dust.
We held them up and nailed them down
and square by square we taped the rooms
against ourselves

But time has shown us when to take our ease.
We sit here now before this fire

in the storm-lulled house
remembering back through the craft
that taught us both
how to see through walls

Cold Carbonara: A Reminiscence

They say
you keep llamas now.
I see them softly munching grass
then moving
like stout ladies in high heels
across the mountain pasture
choosing a new stand of grass
as gracefully as
in those days
we chose new friends

I remember seeing you that first time.
You were sitting on your back stoop
in the Florida panhandle
meditating in Levis and suspenders.
That day you had moved stick by stick
what furniture you owned
out to the garage
to free your mind

It was not comfortable sitting
on your hardwood floor
but it was illuminating

There was a shy-looking woman
in a sailor's shirt
sitting under a hanging lamp
staring into her hands

In three months she would leave you.
You would move the furniture
back into the house
stick by stick
and give up meditation

We drank a lot of beer
I remember
and drove to the Gulf in your
old jeep
listening to Ma Rainey
and her jug band music
not knowing my lover
in the back seat
would leave me in three months
not knowing you would fall in love
with a yuppie lawyer
buy a house and eat red meat

For me it was a year in Italy
where I learned enough of the
language from the grocers on
the Via de Neri to talk
cosmology with the laundress
the one who always filed my white bag
under *"stranieri"*

She said not to worry about
a lost sock
that in the plan of things
if everybody kept bringing back

articles not belonging to them
that eventually and in time
everybody would get back
everything belonging to them

When I returned from my studies
you were meditating on your back porch
having left the mime artist
in Minnesota

We walked to my house
and drank a lot of beer.
MacFall climbed into the
bathtub of dirty water
to play with the rubber duck
the kids had left behind.
Hammer wrote odes in the kitchen
and I finally rode my
unicycle down the hall
but nobody saw
and you fell asleep
on the floor

All night I heard you
eating cold carbonara
out of the refrigerator
and hear you still
and see your dark-eyed llamas
move their soft lips over
tender shots of North Carolina grass

Circus Camp

*For my daughter on her
twenty-first birthday*

It was a hot summer
You were eight then
We lived in the tall house with
no furniture
You slept in the attic
whose sloping sides
tucked you
in at night
You read in bed
by flashlight

That summer
I drove you every day
to circus camp
at the school where I
taught short stories to
short students all day

Late afternoons we would
collapse around the spool
that was our table
drinking lemonade
then you would roller skate
in the living room
until supper

You hadn't said much before
the day we parents
at summer's end
inched ourselves into bleachers
and gazed up to find our children
Miss Sarah cinched you around
your tiny waist
and hoisted you into the sky
I held you in my viewfinder
hands shaking as
calmly you turned
upside down
suspended by one foot
then began to
turn in lazy spirals
the ancient Spanish rope trick
taught to you by strangers
and by your own kid nerve

Sunday Morning

We rose at three
drove up the coast
in your VW van
through rifts of fog
past Pismo Beach
and the lonely red gas station

Oil wells were pumping
remember?
like tall birds drinking
from a deep pool

We climbed in the fat van
up cliffs the color of dead weeds
and down some rutted road until
there was the sea beneath
stirring in her sleep

Hunger began
like a sleepwalker
in my stomach

We rolled up our Levis
grabbed croaker sacks
and tire irons
each of us moving as if
we had done this a thousand
times before

We slid down the gravel cliff
dragging our tools
until the barbed wire
which Ann Martin lifted and held
while the six of us slid one by one
through the breach

and then the shore before us lay
like a woman asleep
we moved with care
pulling sneakered feet
through cold water

You found the first abalone
and yelled so loud it clamped down tight

Ann Martin held her finger to her lip.
I thought of Cary Grant
and the trained feet
of a jewel thief with class
come to steal from Grace Kelly
who always slept with one eye open

We must move quietly in this life
not thinking of the cold salt water
or of the warmth of Grace Kelly's royal breasts
as she breathes softly against hotel pillows

We must think
for a time
only of the iridescent shell

hugged on a black rock
in the dead of morning

Slip your tire iron quickly
under the pink flesh
break the seal
and drop the swag
into your bag

Later, we straggled up the hill
collapsed on the feet of the oaks
and drank cold California wine
from green bottles

Ann Martin made a long table
out of planks and sawhorses

First we pounded the scooped fish thin
tossing the shining empty shells into a pile
then you fried the steaks quick in sparking butter
on a Coleman stove
I tossed salad
pulled the French bread
into hunks
and then we ate —
like pirates
like thieves
like lovers

A few of the publications of
THE NAIAD PRESS, INC.
P.O. Box 10543 ● Tallahassee, Florida 32302
Phone (904) 539-5965
Mail orders welcome. Please include 15% postage.

WOMAN PLUS WOMAN by Dolores Klaich. 300 pp. Supurb
Lesbian overview.   ISBN 0-941483-28-2 $9.95

SLOW DANCING AT MISS POLLY'S by Sheila Ortiz Taylor.
96 pp. Lesbian Poetry   ISBN 0-941483-30-4 $7.95

DOUBLE DAUGHTER by Vicki P. McConnell. 216 pp. A Nyla
Wade Mystery, third in the series.   ISBN 0-941483-26-6 $8.95

HEAVY GILT by Delores Klaich. 192 pp. Lesbian detective/
disappearing homophobes/upper class gay society.
                                               ISBN 0-941483-25-8   8.95

THE FINER GRAIN by Denise Ohio. 216 pp. Brilliant young
college lesbian novel.   ISBN 0-941483-11-8   8.95

THE AMAZON TRAIL by Lee Lynch. 216 pp. Life, travel & lore
of famous lesbian author.   ISBN 0-941483-27-4   8.95

HIGH CONTRAST by Jessie Lattimore. 264 pp. Women of the
Crystal Palace.   ISBN 0-941483-17-7   8.95

OCTOBER OBSESSION by Meredith More. Josie's rich, secret
Lesbian life.   ISBN 0-941483-18-5   8.95

LESBIAN CROSSROADS by Ruth Baetz. 276 pp. Contemporary
Lesbian lives.   ISBN 0-941483-21-5   9.95

BEFORE STONEWALL: THE MAKING OF A GAY AND
LESBIAN COMMUNITY by Andrea Weiss & Greta Schiller.
96 pp., 25 illus.   ISBN 0-941483-20-7   7.95

WE WALK THE BACK OF THE TIGER by Patricia A. Murphy.
192 pp. Romantic Lesbian novel/beginning women's movement.
                                               ISBN 0-941483-13-4   8.95

SUNDAY'S CHILD by Joyce Bright. 216 pp. Lesbian athletics, at
last the novel about sports.   ISBN 0-941483-12-6   8.95

OSTEN'S BAY by Zenobia N. Vole. 204 pp. Sizzling adventure
romance set on Bonaire.   ISBN 0-941483-15-0   8.95

LESSONS IN MURDER by Claire McNab. 216 pp. 1st in a stylish
mystery series.   ISBN 0-941483-14-2   8.95

YELLOWTHROAT by Penny Hayes. 240 pp. Margarita, bandit,
kidnaps Julia.   ISBN 0-941483-10-X   8.95

SAPPHISTRY: THE BOOK OF LESBIAN SEXUALITY by
Pat Califia. 3d edition, revised. 208 pp.   ISBN 0-941483-24-X   8.95

CHERISHED LOVE by Evelyn Kennedy. 192 pp. Erotic
Lesbian love story.   ISBN 0-941483-08-8   8.95

LAST SEPTEMBER by Helen R. Hull. 208 pp. Six stories & a
glorious novella.   ISBN 0-941483-09-6   8.95

THE SECRET IN THE BIRD by Camarin Grae. 312 pp. Striking,
psychological suspense novel.   ISBN 0-941483-05-3   8.95

TO THE LIGHTNING by Catherine Ennis. 208 pp. Romantic
Lesbian 'Robinson Crusoe' adventure.   ISBN 0-941483-06-1   8.95

THE OTHER SIDE OF VENUS by Shirley Verel. 224 pp.
Luminous, romantic love story.   ISBN 0-941483-07-X   8.95

DREAMS AND SWORDS by Katherine V. Forrest. 192 pp.
Romantic, erotic, imaginative stories.   ISBN 0-941483-03-7   8.95

MEMORY BOARD by Jane Rule. 336 pp. Memorable novel
about an aging Lesbian couple.   ISBN 0-941483-02-9   8.95

THE ALWAYS ANONYMOUS BEAST by Lauren Wright
Douglas. 224 pp. A Caitlin Reese mystery. First in a series.
                                      ISBN 0-941483-04-5   8.95

SEARCHING FOR SPRING by Patricia A. Murphy. 224 pp.
Novel about the recovery of love.   ISBN 0-941483-00-2   8.95

DUSTY'S QUEEN OF HEARTS DINER by Lee Lynch. 240 pp.
Romantic blue-collar novel.   ISBN 0-941483-01-0   8.95

PARENTS MATTER by Ann Muller. 240 pp. Parents'
relationships with Lesbian daughters and gay sons.
                                      ISBN 0-930044-91-6   9.95

THE PEARLS by Shelley Smith. 176 pp. Passion and fun in
the Caribbean sun.   ISBN 0-930044-93-2   7.95

MAGDALENA by Sarah Aldridge. 352 pp. Epic Lesbian novel
set on three continents.   ISBN 0-930044-99-1   8.95

THE BLACK AND WHITE OF IT by Ann Allen Shockley.
144 pp. Short stories.   ISBN 0-930044-96-7   7.95

SAY JESUS AND COME TO ME by Ann Allen Shockley. 288
pp. Contemporary romance.   ISBN 0-930044-98-3   8.95

LOVING HER by Ann Allen Shockley. 192 pp. Romantic love
story.   ISBN 0-930044-97-5   7.95

MURDER AT THE NIGHTWOOD BAR by Katherine V.
Forrest. 240 pp. A Kate Delafield mystery. Second in a series.
                                      ISBN 0-930044-92-4   8.95

ZOE'S BOOK by Gail Pass. 224 pp. Passionate, obsessive love
story.   ISBN 0-930044-95-9   7.95

WINGED DANCER by Camarin Grae. 228 pp. Erotic Lesbian
adventure story.   ISBN 0-930044-88-6   8.95

PAZ by Camarin Grae. 336 pp. Romantic Lesbian adventurer
with the power to change the world.   ISBN 0-930044-89-4   8.95

SOUL SNATCHER by Camarin Grae. 224 pp. A puzzle, an
adventure, a mystery — Lesbian romance.   ISBN 0-930044-90-8   8.95

THE LOVE OF GOOD WOMEN by Isabel Miller. 224 pp.
Long-awaited new novel by the author of the beloved *Patience
and Sarah.*   ISBN 0-930044-81-9   8.95

THE HOUSE AT PELHAM FALLS by Brenda Weathers. 240
pp. Suspenseful Lesbian ghost story.   ISBN 0-930044-79-7   7.95

HOME IN YOUR HANDS by Lee Lynch. 240 pp. More stories
from the author of *Old Dyke Tales.*   ISBN 0-930044-80-0   7.95

EACH HAND A MAP by Anita Skeen. 112 pp. Real-life poems
that touch us all.   ISBN 0-930044-82-7   6.95

SURPLUS by Sylvia Stevenson. 342 pp. A classic early Lesbian
novel.   ISBN 0-930044-78-9   7.95

PEMBROKE PARK by Michelle Martin. 256 pp. Derring-do
and daring romance in Regency England.   ISBN 0-930044-77-0   7.95

THE LONG TRAIL by Penny Hayes. 248 pp. Vivid adventures
of two women in love in the old west.   ISBN 0-930044-76-2   8.95

HORIZON OF THE HEART by Shelley Smith. 192 pp. Hot
romance in summertime New England.   ISBN 0-930044-75-4   7.95

AN EMERGENCE OF GREEN by Katherine V. Forrest. 288
pp. Powerful novel of sexual discovery.   ISBN 0-930044-69-X   8.95

THE LESBIAN PERIODICALS INDEX edited by Claire
Potter. 432 pp. Author & subject index.   ISBN 0-930044-74-6   29.95

DESERT OF THE HEART by Jane Rule. 224 pp. A classic;
basis for the movie *Desert Hearts.*   ISBN 0-930044-73-8   7.95

SPRING FORWARD/FALL BACK by Sheila Ortiz Taylor.
288 pp. Literary novel of timeless love.   ISBN 0-930044-70-3   7.95

FOR KEEPS by Elisabeth Nonas. 144 pp. Contemporary novel
about losing and finding love.   ISBN 0-930044-71-1   7.95

TORCHLIGHT TO VALHALLA by Gale Wilhelm. 128 pp.
Classic novel by a great Lesbian writer.   ISBN 0-930044-68-1   7.95

LESBIAN NUNS: BREAKING SILENCE edited by Rosemary
Curb and Nancy Mañahan. 432 pp. Unprecedented autobiographies
of religious life.   ISBN 0-930044-62-2   9.95

THE SWASHBUCKLER by Lee Lynch. 288 pp. Colorful novel
set in Greenwich Village in the sixties.   ISBN 0-930044-66-5   8.95

MISFORTUNE'S FRIEND by Sarah Aldridge. 320 pp. Histori-
cal Lesbian novel set on two continents.   ISBN 0-930044-67-3   7.95

A STUDIO OF ONE'S OWN by Ann Stokes. Edited by
Dolores Klaich. 128 pp. Autobiography.   ISBN 0-930044-64-9   7.95

SEX VARIANT WOMEN IN LITERATURE by Jeannette
Howard Foster. 448 pp. Literary history.   ISBN 0-930044-65-7   8.95

A HOT-EYED MODERATE by Jane Rule. 252 pp. Hard-hitting
essays on gay life; writing; art.   ISBN 0-930044-57-6   7.95

INLAND PASSAGE AND OTHER STORIES by Jane Rule.
288 pp. Wide-ranging new collection.   ISBN 0-930044-56-8   7.95

WE TOO ARE DRIFTING by Gale Wilhelm. 128 pp. Timeless
Lesbian novel, a masterpiece.   ISBN 0-930044-61-4   6.95

AMATEUR CITY by Katherine V. Forrest. 224 pp. A Kate
Delafield mystery. First in a series.   ISBN 0-930044-55-X   7.95

THE SOPHIE HOROWITZ STORY by Sarah Schulman. 176
pp. Engaging novel of madcap intrigue.   ISBN 0-930044-54-1   7.95

THE BURNTON WIDOWS by Vickie P. McConnell. 272 pp. A
Nyla Wade mystery, second in the series.   ISBN 0-930044-52-5   7.95

OLD DYKE TALES by Lee Lynch. 224 pp. Extraordinary
stories of our diverse Lesbian lives.   ISBN 0-930044-51-7   8.95

DAUGHTERS OF A CORAL DAWN by Katherine V. Forrest.
240 pp. Novel set in a Lesbian new world.   ISBN 0-930044-50-9   7.95

THE PRICE OF SALT by Claire Morgan. 288 pp. A milestone
novel, a beloved classic.   ISBN 0-930044-49-5   8.95

AGAINST THE SEASON by Jane Rule. 224 pp. Luminous,
complex novel of interrelationships.   ISBN 0-930044-48-7   8.95

LOVERS IN THE PRESENT AFTERNOON by Kathleen
Fleming. 288 pp. A novel about recovery and growth.
                                             ISBN 0-930044-46-0   8.95

TOOTHPICK HOUSE by Lee Lynch. 264 pp. Love between
two Lesbians of different classes.   ISBN 0-930044-45-2   7.95

MADAME AURORA by Sarah Aldridge. 256 pp. Historical
novel featuring a charismatic "seer."   ISBN 0-930044-44-4   7.95

CURIOUS WINE by Katherine V. Forrest. 176 pp. Passionate
Lesbian love story, a best-seller.   ISBN 0-930044-43-6   8.95

BLACK LESBIAN IN WHITE AMERICA by Anita Cornwell.
141 pp. Stories, essays, autobiography.   ISBN 0-930044-41-X   7.50

CONTRACT WITH THE WORLD by Jane Rule. 340 pp.
Powerful, panoramic novel of gay life.   ISBN 0-930044-28-2   7.95

YANTRAS OF WOMANLOVE by Tee A. Corinne. 64 pp.
Photos by noted Lesbian photographer.   ISBN 0-930044-30-4   6.95

MRS. PORTER'S LETTER by Vicki P. McConnell. 224 pp.
The first Nyla Wade mystery.   ISBN 0-930044-29-0   7.95

TO THE CLEVELAND STATION by Carol Anne Douglas.
192 pp. Interracial Lesbian love story.   ISBN 0-930044-27-4   6.95

THE NESTING PLACE by Sarah Aldridge. 224 pp. A
three-woman triangle—love conquers all!   ISBN 0-930044-26-6   7.95

THIS IS NOT FOR YOU by Jane Rule. 284 pp. A letter to a
beloved is also an intricate novel.   ISBN 0-930044-25-8   8.95

FAULTLINE by Sheila Ortiz Taylor. 140 pp. Warm, funny,
literate story of a startling family.   ISBN 0-930044-24-X   6.95

THE LESBIAN IN LITERATURE by Barbara Grier. 3d ed.
Foreword by Maida Tilchen. 240 pp. Comprehensive bibliography.
Literary ratings; rare photos.   ISBN 0-930044-23-1   7.95

ANNA'S COUNTRY by Elizabeth Lang. 208 pp. A woman
finds her Lesbian identity.   ISBN 0-930044-19-3   6.95

PRISM by Valerie Taylor. 158 pp. A love affair between two
women in their sixties.   ISBN 0-930044-18-5   6.95

BLACK LESBIANS: AN ANNOTATED BIBLIOGRAPHY
compiled by J. R. Roberts. Foreword by Barbara Smith. 112 pp.
Award-winning bibliography.   ISBN 0-930044-21-5   5.95

THE MARQUISE AND THE NOVICE by Victoria Ramstetter.
108 pp. A Lesbian Gothic novel.   ISBN 0-930044-16-9   4.95

OUTLANDER by Jane Rule. 207 pp. Short stories and essays
by one of our finest writers.   ISBN 0-930044-17-7   6.95

ALL TRUE LOVERS by Sarah Aldridge. 292 pp. Romantic
novel set in the 1930s and 1940s.   ISBN 0-930044-10-X   7.95

A WOMAN APPEARED TO ME by Renee Vivien. 65 pp. A
classic; translated by Jeannette H. Foster.   ISBN 0-930044-06-1   5.00

CYTHEREA'S BREATH by Sarah Aldridge. 240 pp. Romantic
novel about women's entrance into medicine.
                                             ISBN 0-930044-02-9   6.95

TOTTIE by Sarah Aldridge. 181 pp. Lesbian romance in the
turmoil of the sixties.   ISBN 0-930044-01-0   6.95

THE LATECOMER by Sarah Aldridge. 107 pp. A delicate love
story.   ISBN 0-930044-00-2   5.00

ODD GIRL OUT by Ann Bannon.   ISBN 0-930044-83-5   5.95

I AM A WOMAN by Ann Bannon.   ISBN 0-930044-84-3   5.95

WOMEN IN THE SHADOWS by Ann Bannon.
                                             ISBN 0-930044-85-1   5.95

JOURNEY TO A WOMAN by Ann Bannon.
                                             ISBN 0-930044-86-X   5.95

BEEBO BRINKER by Ann Bannon.   ISBN 0-930044-87-8   5.95
          Legendary novels written in the fifties and sixties,
          set in the gay mecca of Greenwich Village.

VOLUTE BOOKS

JOURNEY TO FULFILLMENT   Early classics by Valerie   3.95

| A WORLD WITHOUT MEN | Taylor: The Erika Frohmann | 3.95 |
| RETURN TO LESBOS | series. | 3.95 |

These are just a few of the many Naiad Press titles — we are the oldest and largest lesbian/feminist publishing company in the world. Please request a complete catalog. We offer personal service; we encourage and welcome direct mail orders from individuals who have limited access to bookstores carrying our publications.